contents

Before you start

About this book

Clay is a wonderful material for making things.
You can poke, prod, squeeze, squash, roll, pinch
and join it, using just your fingers and thumbs.
Every project in this book is simple to make and
will give you practice in basic techniques of
working with clay. Enjoy making a ladybird box,
a puppet, a board game, a lion's head and
many more exciting ideas.

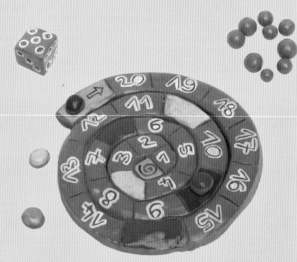

Tools and materials

Make the projects from terracotta – a reddish-
brown clay. You can paint and varnish the clay
(with PVA glue) once it is dry but it will not be
waterproof, so avoid getting your clay models too
wet. You could also use air-hardening clay. It is
smoother and denser than terracotta and may
harden before you have finished working with it.

You need a wooden board to work on, a knife for
cutting, and a rolling pin and hessian (strong, thick
fabric) for making slabs. A hand-held water spray
is useful for keeping clay soft. To make **clay slip** for
joining slabs: mix scraps of dry clay with water. Let
it stand until the clay breaks down. Strain off extra
water, leaving a creamy mixture. Keep the mixture
in a plastic box with a lid.

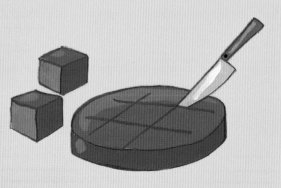

Make It Yourself

with clay

W
FRANKLIN WATTS
LONDON · SYDNEY

This edition published in 2006 by
Franklin Watts
338 Euston Road
London NW1 3BH

Franklin Watts Australia
Hachette Children's Books
Level 17/207 Kent Street
Sydney NSW 2000

Originally published by
Casterman, Belgium
Original edition © Casterman 1999
English edition © Franklin Watts 2006

Text, illustrations and photography:
  Godeleine de Rosamel
Design: Dominique Mazy
Translation: Ruth Thomson

ISBN-10: 0 7496 6909 8
ISBN-13: 978 0 7496 6909 6

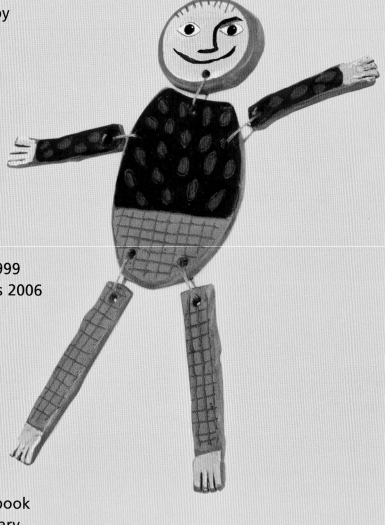

A CIP catalogue record for this book
is available from the British Library.

Dewey Classification: 738.1'2

Printed in China

working with clay

• Make sure the clay is not too sticky or too firm to work with.
• Wrap finished work loosely in a plastic bag, so that it does not dry too quickly, or it may crack.
• Wrap spare clay tightly in polythene so that it does not go hard.

Rolling out a slab

Cover a board with canvas or hessian. Flatten a lump of clay with your hands. Then stand up to roll it out, so you can push down hard on the rolling pin. Roll the clay to and fro to make an even slab. Turn it over to peel off the hessian.

Rolling coils

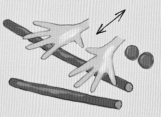

Squeeze a lump of soft clay (the size of an orange) into a sausage shape. Roll it back and forth with your *whole* hand. Roll gently, so that you do not flatten the coil. Move your hands sideways to make the coil even. Be careful not to make coils too thin, or they will break.

Joining clay

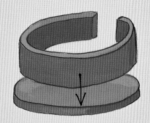

Use a knife tip to score (make criss-cross lines on) the edges to be joined. Then paint them with clay slip (see page 6). Press the edges together and smooth them inside and out.

Learning logos

The activities in the book provide practice in different skills, identified by the logos below.

An activity practising imagination and creativity

An activity practising fine motor control

An activity involving the notion of balance

An activity involving picturing the body

An activity practising pattern making

coaster

clay ● rolling pin ● knife ● shallow dish
paintbrush ● gouche paints ● PVA glue or varnish

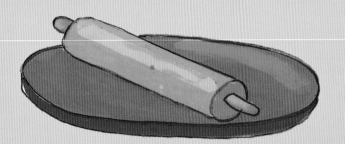

1 Roll out a slab of clay with a rolling pin.

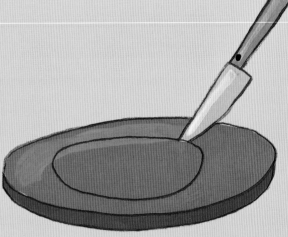

2 Cut out a circle with a knife.

3 Shape the circle in a dish, smoothing out the edges all the way round.

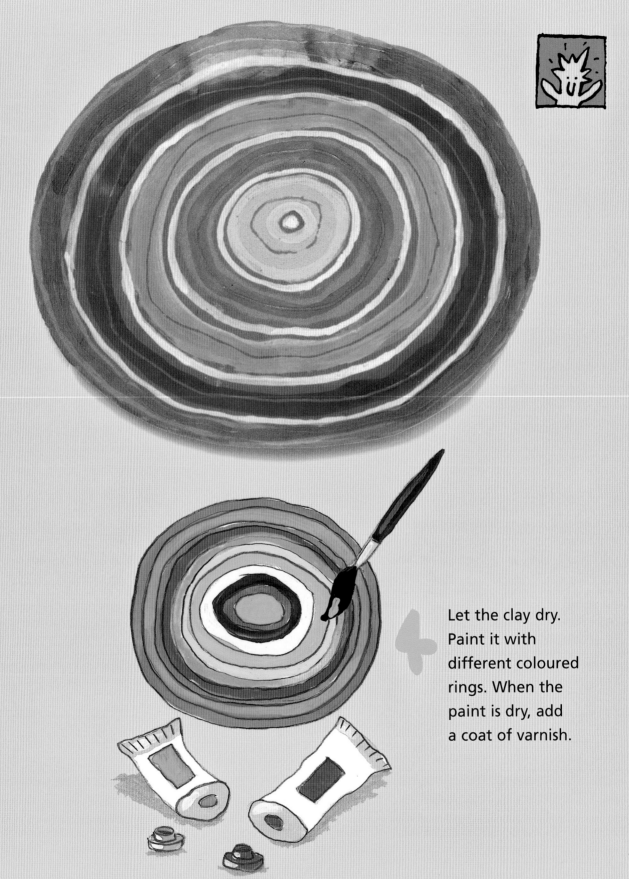

Let the clay dry.
Paint it with
different coloured
rings. When the
paint is dry, add
a coat of varnish.

Marbles and dice

clay ● rolling pin ● knife ● pencil
gouache paints ● paintbrush ● PVA glue or varnish

1 Roll small lumps of clay between your hands to make balls for marbles.

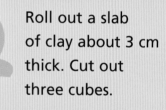

2 Roll out a slab of clay about 3 cm thick. Cut out three cubes.

3 cm

3 Mark and press into the clay a number or dot on each face of the dice.

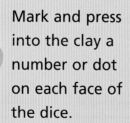

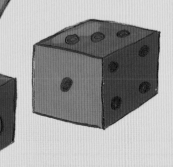

When the clay is dry, paint the dots or numbers on the dice with white paint.

Varnish the marbles and dice once the paint is dry.

Make up some games to play with your marbles and dice.

Ladybird box

clay ● rolling pin ● knife ● pencil ● gouache paints
paintbrush ● PVA glue or varnish ● wire ● pliers

1 Roll out two slabs of clay. Cut out two circles both the same size. Cut a clay strip, long enough to fit around a circle.

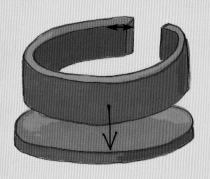

2 Make a box base by joining the strip to one of the circles (see page 7).

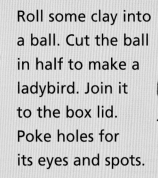

3 Roll some clay into a ball. Cut the ball in half to make a ladybird. Join it to the box lid. Poke holes for its eyes and spots.

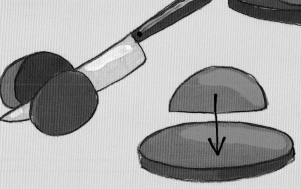

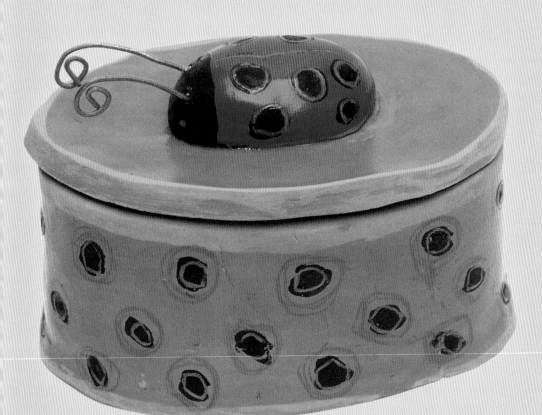

Cut two pieces of wire and curl one end. Push the other end into the ladybird's head to make antennae. Once the clay is dry, paint and varnish the ladybird and the box.

Use the box to keep jewellery or small objects in.

Noughts and crosses

clay ● rolling pin ● knife ● ruler ● pencil
gouache paints ● paintbrush ● PVA glue or varnish

1 Roll out a slab of clay. Cut out a board, sized 15 x 15 cm.

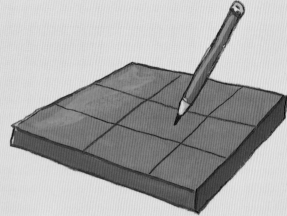

2 Divide the board into nine 5 cm squares, scratching lines on it with a pencil.

3 Roll out another slab of clay. Cut out ten 5 cm squares. Mark X on five of the small squares and 0 on the other five.

Once the clay is dry, paint both the board and all the playing pieces. Varnish them when the paint is dry.

Challenge someone to a game!

puppet

clay ● rolling pin ● knife ● pencil ● gouache paints
paintbrush ● PVA glue or varnish ● thin round elastic

1. Roll out a large slab of clay. Cut out a head, a body, two arms and legs.

2. Mark the puppet's face with a pencil. Poke holes in each piece in the positions shown below.

3. Leave the clay to dry. Then paint and varnish all the puppet pieces.

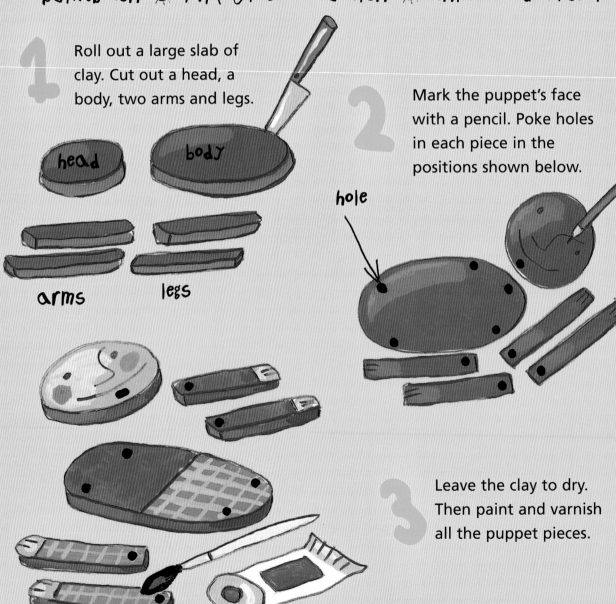

head

body

arms

legs

hole

16

Cut five pieces of elastic. Thread each one through the holes to join the head, arms and legs to the body. Knot the ends together.

Act out a play with your puppet!

Flowers

clay ● rolling pin ● Knife ● pencil ● gouache paints
paintbrush ● PVA glue or varnish ● thin wire
pliers ● flowerpot ● pebbles

1 Roll out a slab of clay. Cut out different flower shapes.

2 Using a pencil, score the centre of each flower with spots, squares or a spiral. Poke a small hole in one side of each flower.

3 Leave the clay to dry, then paint each flower differently.

Varnish all of them when the paint is dry.

Cut two lengths of wire for each flower. Twist two pieces together to make each stem. Glue a stem into the hole in each flower.

Stand the flowers in a flowerpot full of garden pebbles.

19

Board game

clay ● knife ● pencil ● gouache paints
paintbrush ● PVA glue or varnish

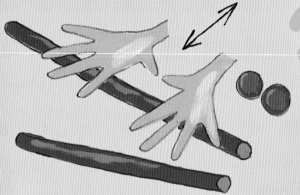

1 Roll out several long clay sausage shapes, all the same thickness. Also roll two small balls of clay.

2 Make a spiral with the sausage shapes, joining the ends together (see page 7). Flatten the spiral into a board. Squash the balls and cut them in half.

3 Using a pencil, divide the spiral into squares and number them as you wish. Leave every fifth square blank. Leave the clay to dry.

playing pieces

HOW TO PLAY

• Decide in advance what the coloured squares mean – for example, yellow squares might mean move forward two squares; red squares might mean move back one square. Invent new rules each time you play.

• Take it in turns to throw the dice. Move forward the same number of squares as shown on the dice.

• The first player to reach the centre wins.

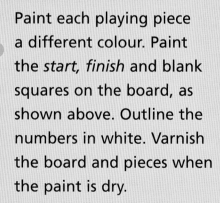

Paint each playing piece a different colour. Paint the *start, finish* and blank squares on the board, as shown above. Outline the numbers in white. Varnish the board and pieces when the paint is dry.

caterpillar pot

clay ● rolling pin ● knife ● pencil
gouache paints ● paintbrush ● wire ● pliers

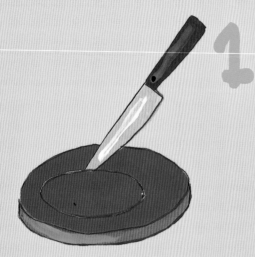

1 Roll out a slab of clay. Cut out a circle to make the base.

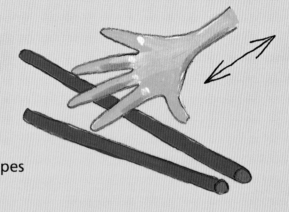

2 Roll out several long sausage shapes of clay.

3 Coil the sausage shapes in a spiral to make the walls of the pot. Press them firmly together. Join the walls to the base (see page 7).

Model a caterpillar's head at the top. Draw its eyes and mouth. Poke two holes on top of its head.

Leave the clay to dry. Paint the pot and give the caterpillar a funny expression.

Cut two lengths of wire. Curl them at one end. Glue and push the other end into the holes on the caterpillar's head for antennae.

candlesticks

clay ● rolling pin ● tumbler ● candles
PVA glue or varnish

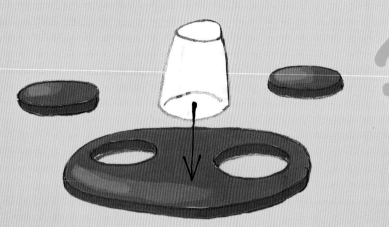

1 Roll out a slab of clay. Press out three circles, using a tumbler turned upside-down.

2 Roll three balls of clay in your hands.

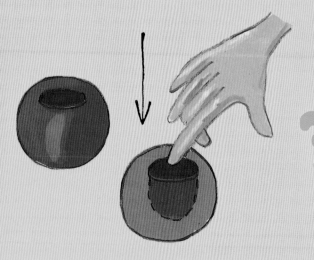

3 Press your forefinger halfway down each ball, making a hole big enough for the base of a candle.

Join each ball to one of the clay circles (see page 7) to make a candlestick. Once the clay is dry, varnish it.

Lion's head

clay ● rolling pin ● knife ● pencil ● gouche paint
paintbrush ● PVA glue or varnish ● raffia, wool or string

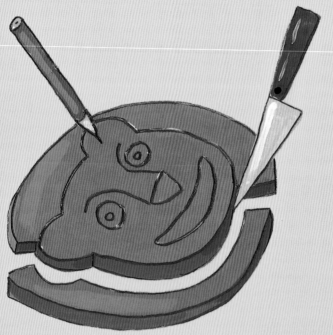

1 Roll out a slab of clay. Draw a lion's head on it.

Cut out the outline of the head with a knife.

2 Add on extra details, such as a big nose or sharp teeth.

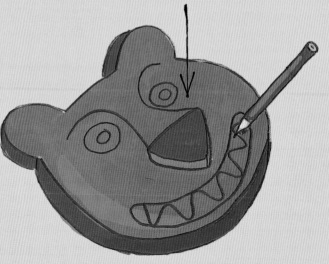

3 Pierce holes at regular intervals around the outside of the head (but not on the ears). Leave the clay to dry.

4 Paint and varnish the lion. Knot a piece of raffia, wool or string through each of the holes.

Bird

clay ● feathers ● gouche paint
paintbrush ● PVA glue or varnish

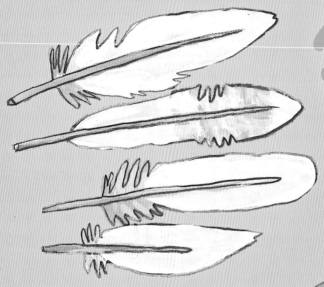

1 Collect some bird feathers.

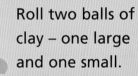

2 Roll two balls of clay – one large and one small.

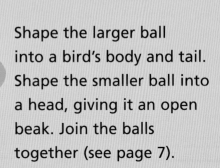

3 Shape the larger ball into a bird's body and tail. Shape the smaller ball into a head, giving it an open beak. Join the balls together (see page 7).

Push the feathers into
the clay to make a pair
of wings and a tail.
Leave the clay to dry.
Paint it. Varnish the bird
when the paint is dry.

If your bird's feathers
fall out, glue them back
in position.

index

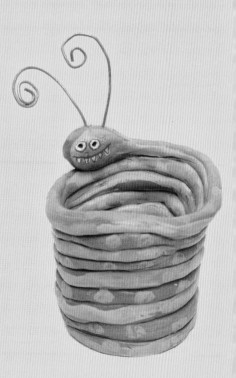